Blood Is Red ... So Am I

Annie Lou Alexander

VANTAGE PRESS
New York

Cover design by Susan Thomas

FIRST EDITION

All rights reserved, including the right of
reproduction in whole or in part in any form.

Copyright © 2007 by Annie Lou Alexander

Published by Vantage Press, Inc.
419 Park Ave. South, New York, NY 10016

Manufactured in the United States of America
ISBN: 978-0-533-15226-1

Library of Congress Catalog Card No.: 2005903396

0 9 8 7 6 5 4 3 2 1

Contents

1. Vacation? What's That? — 1
2. Indian Fingernails — 8
3. Blood Is Red . . . So Am I — 12
4. Kuthla Smiled at Me — 21
5. I Will Always Fear Rodents — 26
6. Snake, Annie Lou! — 30
7. River Rock Wars at Celilo Falls — 33
8. The Drowning — 36
9. Salmon Feast at Celilo Falls — 39
10. Swimming in the Rain — 43
11. They Took Our Thunder — 46

1
Vacation? What's That?

The other students who weren't Native Americans talked about their families going on vacations every summer or over the winter break. They took cross-country hiking trips during part of the summer, sunbathed in Hawaii, or got in some skiing at local mountain passes and a few went to Sun Valley, Idaho over the Christmas and New Year's holidays. They showed me out-of-focus, jerky movies they took on these trips from round metal reels shown on white screens in their living rooms where all the furnishings matched. Their parents always asked me where my family went on our vacations.

"Our what? Vacations?"

I told them I guess we were always on vacation in the summers of the late 50s and early 60s. In the winter and summer on weekends, we ice fished in lakes on the Colville Indian Reservation where my mother was born. We also hunted for deer and elk, butchering and drying the meat over open fires in the mountains before we came home. I had such good times.

After The Dalles Dam was completed on the Columbia River in March, 1957, the floodgates were closed and the river covered ancient Celilo Falls and our yearly summer fishing village on the Oregon side. My parents, with tears in their eyes, told us that we would never see Celilo Falls or the salmon jump up into our fishing nets there again. In their voices, it was like a close relative had died. They took me that day to go watch with a group of other Indians as the dammed-up Columbia River rose and covered up our Celilo Falls and beloved summer homes. That day remains in my heart and memory as a sad day.

Following that sad year (1957) in my life, Indian families changed their summer migration that began when school let out for the summer vacation from moving to Celilo Falls for commercial fishing just as the summer fishing season opened to following the crops in Washington and Oregon states.

Usually two or three families traveled together, loading camping gear in trucks and Dad's trusty, maroon Studebaker.

After Celilo was flooded, and school let out for the summer in June, we had less than two weeks before we had to pack up and move to pick cherries. We camped at the orchards located south, above the Dalles, Oregon. The season lasted about three weeks. Dad stayed at home in Wapato because he had a job with the BIA Reclamation Bureau and came to check on us on his payday weekend or when he had *vacation* time. Other Indian families moved to the same place, so we always had relatives and friends our age from the reservation for company and to get in trouble with. Being typical kids, we sneaked over to the water faucet in the evening and smoked cigarettes taken, unbeknownst to the grown-ups, from their packs before we had to go to bed. When and if we got caught, we had to pack all the water, and clean camp until we moved again! We always got a verbal then a physical thrashing from the whip man (invited by our parents) to "put us on the right path." As far as I can reason, those whippings didn't hurt us psychologically one bit. We were always lectured and told what we were being punished for before the whip, which we had to cut ourselves, was taken out.

When weekends rolled around, we washed our hair at the faucet and bathed in camp with soapy wash cloths then rinsed squeaky-clean with buckets of cold water. My folks called this our "birdbaths." Then we drew our pay and went into The Dalles to eat Chinese food and shop at the Goodwill. We didn't want a whole lot, just to get what we needed and a short break from working for a couple of days was okay with us. Sometimes on weekends we got out our suitcases of buckskin outfits and eagle feathers to travel to a local pow wow to dress up, dance, and visit old friends and relatives. Our regalia or outfits were always packed and ready for use, except when we went camping in the mountains on the reservation. Wherever we went, the women always had a bead-working project or repairing of some kind going on in their spare time.

When the cherry picking season was over, we'd move home for about two weeks and buy new jars with lids so Mamma could preserve the leftover cherries we brought home. The farmer was usually happy with our work, plus the season was prosperous, so he let us take home as much as we wanted. In the winter we loved eating homemade canned fruit picked the summer before, especially with Mamma's moist, yellow cake made from scratch.

When the first part of July rolled around, Mamma and Dad would pack us up again to go pick raspberries for three weeks close to Gresham, Oregon. Mamma was usually the one who would drive with us kids and Dad would come over later, every two weeks because of his job. The same families we worked with at The Dalles would also show up and we all set up camp like before. The owner of one particular raspberry field was named Mr. Edmonds. He knew most of the Indian families and would tell us who was already there and who hadn't shown up yet.

There was a store nearby where we bribed my older brother to buy us a pack of cigarettes. I was always searched by Mamma, so I had my friend Joanne keep the cigarettes for us and she would meet us in the evenings. I knew Mr. Edmonds was the one who told my folks we sneaked those cigarettes between the rows of raspberries.

Mr. Edmonds would always drop by in the early evenings just to share a piece of fry bread with commodity peanut butter and Mamma's fresh raspberry jam with us. Mamma always gave him a few extra pieces for his breakfast or lunch the next day. He developed a strong fondness for fry bread and had Mamma show his daughter-in-law how to make it in his own kitchen. Mamma said Greta, his daughter-in-law, didn't quite get it right but she made pretty good fry bread. Mr. Edmonds still liked Mamma's bread best. He said Greta ruined the bread when she experimented—adding stuff like cinnamon, buttermilk, and various other ingredients. Mr. Edmonds said he was "ruint" when he first tasted Mamma's brand of delicious fry bread.

The big city of Portland, Oregon was close enough so that we went to movies there, or swimming at nearby Dodge Park, and we had many good gooshy raspberry fights to burn off mischievous energy! There was an AM radio station that played the best R & R called KISN (the kissin' station). My sister Joyce's portable radio rocked the berry patch to songs sung by Elvis Presley, Ritchie Valens, Bill Haley and his Comets, and Fats Domino.

When raspberry picking season was over and Mamma had canned a few dozen jars for winter, we moved home again for a week or two.

Now it was the first part of August, so we got ready to

go camping again, on the reservation up in the mountains to pick our beloved huckleberries for about three weeks. We made periodic trips back home or to the nearest town of Glenwood, Washington for fresh supplies.

Each and every morning from camp, we looked southwest at Mt. Adams—a beautiful, majestic, moving sight that lifted my soul. The view was so sharp and crystal clear. From Wapato we'd look west at Mt. Adams and see it through a thin haze with the familiar pattern in the mountain of a horse running northward with its mane flying. It was carved by nature in granite in the east side of the mountain. I used to think it was a gift for our eyes, a picture of art from the Creator.

Our fathers, uncles, brothers, the hunters, would pick a day to go hunting for deer or elk. We cut up the meat in strips for drying over a fire at camp. The hide was rolled up and saved to work on at home. We fished in nearby Mt. Adams and Howard Lake for fresh trout. Everything we ate in the mountains tasted so good, even creamed corn and yucky peas!

Other families from the reservation had their camps nearby, just like when we picked cherries and raspberries. This was the final trek of our <u>vacation.</u> The other kids would come to our camp, or we went to theirs. We'd chase chattering chipmunks, never catching one. Once, my cousin Melvin grabbed one by its tail and all the hair came off. It ran up a tree with a bright pink tail, stripped clean! When we got tired of that, we bent small pine trees, jumping up and down on them, riding them like wild broncs. We'd get thrown off, of course, and jump on another "horse."

We didn't get into trouble here as much as we ordinarily did because we had so much fun exploring everywhere and walking for miles with a basket woven of cedar tied around our waists. We filled the baskets and ate huckleberries whenever we wanted every day. We usually got teased by the grown-ups for coming back with blue-tinged tongues and lips. We weren't supposed to eat one berry until we filled our baskets and brought it back to camp with huckleberry branches and leaves tied over the top. Well, yeah, we knew that traditional rule but we didn't always follow it. Being kids, it was impossible.

When huckleberry season was over and we had all the berries and venison we needed, we'd strike camp and move home so Mamma could preserve and make a few jars of her fabulous huckleberry jam. Of course we also had to finish bagging and freezing the dried deer and elk meat for the winter. After that we'd soak the hides for a few days, then it was time to laboriously scrape off the hair and three thin layers of fibrous tissue. Next we stretched the wet, softened hide in all directions until it was dried. During this process we seasoned the hide by rubbing in rotten brains of the deer or elk. The *really* putrid stuff (sometimes a few months' old) is the best you can get! This helped the hide dry into a smelly, velvety softness before we smoked-tanned it into various shades of rich, cinnamon brown. Like human fingerprints, each hide comes out in different shades, no two are ever alike, but some come close. I guess the brains are like fine wine, we get the nutrients at their peak from "aged" brains and saturate them into every fiber of the hide to make the finished buckskin soft, but very durable.

We use buckskins for many things in our culture, such as: traditional clothing, decoration, bags of all kinds for both men and women, ties in our braids, and rope. We don't make tipis out of buckskin anymore, but we still make and wear moccasins with leggings for ceremonies.

It takes a lot of elbow grease to rub and scrape the oily, squishy brains into the hide, similar to putting butter on bread, but fifty times harder. The smell, scraping and stretching those stinky hides was the only part of my summer <u>vacation</u> I detested!

By this time we had a couple of days and Labor Day weekend left before we had to start back to school for fall. Now I ask you—how could I tell the non-Native Americans at school about my vacation after hearing about the wonderful places they went and what they did? To me and my Indian people, our summer break sounded perfect. Of course, I had to work hard and never got to sun on the Pacific beach in Hawaii, go water skiing, or shake Goofy's hand at Disneyland. (He's real, you know. My sister Joyce saw him once!)

At school that fall, each student had to get up and tell the class about their summer. In a shorter version, I told the class about what I just wrote here. A few students told me it sounded like I had a great time and they were envious. My fourth-grade teacher, Mrs. Burke, was appalled and told me that such cruel treatment wasn't fair of my parents. I didn't know how to answer her, so I sat down. *What wasn't fair?* I had so much fun, I could hardly wait for next year. I wouldn't have it any other way. It was an unforgettable and most wonderful time to be growing up.

2
Indian Fingernails

My ordinary life at home didn't seem to be quite like some of the other students in my school at Wapato, Washington on the Yakama Indian Reservation in the 50s and early 60s. When I was growing up during my elementary school years, my classmates of different nationalities told me what their home life was like, and I couldn't help but to compare their lives with mine.

I remember our neighbors, the Filipinos across the vast cucumber, tomato, and corn fields from us, telling me about their families all bathing together in a huge square steel tub enclosed inside a homemade bathhouse. They made a small fire under the tub outside to heat the water inside. When we played together at their house, they showed me that strange "bathtub." I laughed at such a crazy thing—my Filipino playmates didn't even smile back, they stood there looking at me with emotionless faces.

Now being Native American, we took spiritual cleansing sweat baths, separately from the men. The men always went in first unless there was another sweat lodge built just for the women. We heated lava rocks gathered near the mountains in a fire then placed them in the sweat lodge in a pit. We crawled inside from right to the left and sat in a circle and the leader, the first one in, splashed water boiled with sage on the rocks a sacred number of times, usually from three to five times. We prayed in the darkened, steamy lodge with cedar and other blessing herbs placed on the red-hot rocks. It was aromatherapy. When we came out, we splashed a lot of cold water on ourselves to rinse off. I was told the cold water closed our pores.

The Filipinos couldn't understand how we withstood extremes from near-scalding steam then splashing on ice-cold water, especially in the winter. I guess it was because we had been doing it since we were toddlers, the cold water hardly bothered us.

The Filipinos had huge dinners with whole pigs roasted in pits covered on top and bottom with leaves, canvas, rocks and earth. I recall that they ate deliciously fragrant rice at every meal. Their kitchen always had a long, uncluttered table for students to do their homework in the afternoons and evenings. How I longed for that table to do my homework, and especially to write my poems and thoughts down on paper. I usually did my homework and writing outside under the tree or in the nearby woods sitting up in my favorite cottonwood tree branch shaped like a small armchair. The fresh air and sounds of nature seemed to calm and inspire me at the same time.

Mamma always had bread rising, cakes cooling, or visitors sitting around our kitchen table drinking coffee and eating fresh homemade bread or pie. Our kitchen table was hardly ever empty or uncluttered. There were always people around the kitchen table doing some kind of sewing project, cleaning, or a cooking activity going on from dawn to dusk, and usually long after I was asleep. Whatever went on in my young life seemed to begin and end in our kitchen.

The Mexicans in my class told me about how hard they, their parents, and relatives labored on the local farms, fields, and orchards. Whole families pooled their money to buy homes, pick-ups and food. They were strongly family oriented and usually stayed in one house, sharing living expenses. They lived on the wrong side of town, but wore the latest-style clothes, and the girls wore the nicest shoes I ever saw. I used to wish I had a pair of those shiny patent-leather shoes and gorgeous twin-sweater sets the girls wore. They were handsome people, especially the older ones. It seemed to me as if they were made for their clothes.

When I stayed overnight with my friends Vicenta or Esperanza, I liked to listen to them and their family talk animatedly in their language. I only understood a word or two, but I liked listening, they were such cheerful people. Since then, I have never eaten anything as tasty as their tamales or Esperanza's grandmother's molé chicken, which is boiled with Mexican seasonings then baked smothered with a spicy chocolate sauce.

The Japanese girls and boys were polite, soft-spoken, and always admiring my long, strong "Indian fingernails" they called them. They had pale, soft nails and kept them clipped short. A classmate, Mai, brought a bottle of her older cousin See's orange-red nail polish to school and painted my nails on the playground during lunch recess. She told me she wished she had my nails and invited me to spend the night whenever I wanted my nails redone. I did, and couldn't get over how neat and practically sterile their kitchen was. Everything was put away out of sight. It reminded me of a hospital and looked like the lovely make-believe kitchens in our black-and-white televisions; as if nobody ever cooked in there.

In our kitchen, Mamma had all her utensils hung out where she could reach them right away. Her spices lined the back of the stove, the salt, pepper, and sugar bowls were always in the middle of the table along with a jar of huckleberry jam, peanut butter and freshly baked or fry bread for whoever wanted to make a snack. Mai said her family only ate at meal times and usually didn't have between-meal snacks! It would be years before I envied their way of eating, I certainly didn't then.

Our Indian kitchens were like Grand Central Station. Neighbors, travelers, or anyone was welcome to whatever we had. The elders drilled into our heads that whatever you shared with others would come back to you even more.

Kitchens were the main gathering place of our people when I was growing up and that hasn't changed. I believe those gatherings helped us with our sorrow over the flooding of Celilo Falls. We shared good and bad news with each other over mugs of huckleberry or princess pine tea (our Indian tea) and strong coffee. When there was a birthday dinner, Mamma had me put together a cloth bundle of handkerchiefs and socks to pass out to the men and boys. She bought usable trinkets and silky scarves to give the women and girls, and usually picked up sweets and small, noiseless toys for the children. Each Indian family keeps a stash of small "give-away" items like these on hand for gifts. Everybody gets a present at someone's birthday, and the giver always gets back more, it's true. This has always been our custom, giving from the heart.

3
Blood Is Red . . . So Am I

I was five years old when I cut my hand on a brown beer bottle while mud crawling in the Columbia River at Celilo Falls, Oregon that summer in July, 1948. Mamma didn't allow me to swim in the deep water that day because I had to watch my little sister Joyce and brother Earl Jr. because they couldn't swim yet. I was showing them the way to mud crawl on their hands and knees in the shallow water. Joyce was a toddler, and Earl Jr. was almost ten months old, he crawled all over the place. Close by, Mamma was scrubbing diapers on a wash board in a pail with a bar of Ivory soap. She was going to finish washing the diapers in hot water and bleach at The Dalles in those big machines at the laundromat. That's why we were at the river, to cool off the babies before we went into town.

I felt a painful prick on my left palm and jumped up; when I saw the blood gushing I stated crying. Mamma told me to close my hand a couple of times and squeeze, then she cleaned the cut with the bar of soap and our drinking water. She ripped up a clean, dry diaper and made a bandage for my hand. When the bleeding stopped, I examined the wound under the blood-soaked diaper bandage and shuddered. I asked Mamma, "Where does so much blood come from?" It wasn't the first time I'd seen fresh blood, it's just that I never asked about it before.

She started gently tapping a drumbeat on my chest.

"Blood is red like us Indians. It comes from our heart, pumping life—ta tum, ta tum, ta tum."

"Mamma, that's the same beat for our Circle Dance."

"Yes, Annie Lou, I know. Well, blood goes through our whole body, keeping us alive. When our heart stops pumping blood, we die. You must always take care of your wounds and cuts so they don't get germs or poison will set in. When poison from an infection gets into your blood it flows back to the heart, and kills you very quickly."

She swept her right hand, palm down, from left to right very swiftly. To me, that meant the end, to stop, and in this case—death.

If anything, that bit of information and advice stayed with me the rest of my life.

I remembered when my brother Earl Jr. was born, almost a year before, at the Dalles Hospital in early October. I woke up that morning and immediately wondered where Mamma was because I sensed she was gone. She was always around, ever since I could remember. I felt an almost painful loss because she wasn't there when I woke up. That was because, whenever an especially bad dream woke me up, I cried aloud just so Mamma would appear next to my cot; only then, would I feel safe, and fall back to sleep.

"Where's Mamma?"

Dad told me.

"She went to the hospital when you were sleeping to get our new baby."

While that was sinking in, he started cooking my favorite breakfast of bacon, fried potatoes, and eggs in the same pan on the two-burner hot plate. I liked how all the food took on the salty, mild smoke flavor of bacon. With breakfast, Dad had his usual black coffee and I drank water. Water was kept in three large aluminum cans dairy farmers used for storing milk by our door. There was a big well with a faucet at the fish-and-ice warehouse up the hill where we filled the cans with fresh water every other day. The whole village got their water at that large warehouse.

After we ate, Dad heated two pans of water so we could wash the dishes together. We did this after each meal. He said we had to keep everything put up and clean, no leftovers or scraps, so the rats wouldn't come around. I saw rats scurrying around and fighting sometimes at the warehouse where ice, large fish boxes, and marine/boating equipment were kept.

When Joyce woke up, Dad fed her milk and cereal, then bathed and changed her. I pushed a huge broom and wet mop around the floor and put away our dishes and silverware in wooden lockers. I put the butter, eggs, and milk in the large ice chest. When Joyce was really little, I learned to make her formula in a bottle. I poured one ounce of Karo syrup, one ounce of Carnation canned milk and six ounces of boiled water that had been cooled a little, from a green thermos. For measuring the correct amounts, I used the raised numbers and lines on the bottle like Mamma showed me. I set Joyce's prepared bottle on the table. It was easier now because she drank cold milk poured out of a bottle. Sometimes we gave her milk in a cup because she was eating solid food now. She was tiny, but very strong and healthy, Dad said.

With Joyce under one arm, Dad picked up the bottle before putting her down with it in the hammock-type swing he'd made with Mom's patchwork quilt and two ropes hanging over their bed from ceiling rafters. The safety belt tied around Joyce's middle was a long, colorful yarn belt Mamma had knitted. Dad would have to make another swing for my new baby brother or sister because I didn't think Joyce would give up her beloved swing so easy. Dad said Joyce gave them a lot of trouble when they stopped putting her in her last cradleboard when she turned one, so he made her the swing. Mamma must have already taken the new turquoise cradleboard to the hospital with her because I didn't see it on the tiny corner table where she sewed by the south window. She had an old lamp she bought in a second hand store that she packed every time we moved here to Celilo Falls and back to Wapato after the summer and early fall fishing season was over. The guy who sold it to her for two dollars said it was called a bank teller's lamp, and all it needed was a new bulb. I told Dad when I grew up, I wanted to own one just like it, just because Mamma had one.

"Dad, can I go swimming for awhile?"

"Yeah, go ahead. Here, take these soiled diapers to rinse, then we'll wash them in The Dalles at the laundromat when we go see Mamma and your new little brother this afternoon."

A new baby brother! Until then I didn't know what I had.

"Does he have a name, Dad?"

"Yeah, your mom named him Earl Wahpat Jr., after me. He's my first son, you know."

"Oh-h-h, I didn't know you had a name, Dad."

He grinned at me. "I sure do, everyone does, Annie Lou."

"Okay, Dad, I always believe you."

I took the metal bucket of soiled diapers and headed down the hill to the river. Maybe some other kids will be swimming already. I was usually there first, though. I hoped Lois, or Wanda were there. They were my favorite ones to swim with because they weren't scared of the deep water. I liked to swim with Mavis and Florence too because they had such good stories to tell. They told me about the "snake flowers." Those are the ones with tiny, white clusters of white petals and long velvety green stems. They grow wild all over where it's hot, rocky, and arid. The elders said if you picked them, the snakes would come around you. I asked Mamma about that, and she told me.

"I don't know, Annie Lou, this is the Yakamas' territory, and they have different ways from the Colvilles' where you and I are from. Your dad will know, ask him. You pay attention too, whenever an elder or anyone shares something like that with you, respect each other like all Indians are supposed to."

I got to the river and didn't see anyone but an elderly couple. The old man was cleaning a salmon, standing in the river. I didn't know their names but had seen them at the secondhand store and the Granada theater in The Dalles. They smiled and called me over. I walked closer and smiled shyly. They both had long, thin, mostly white braids and faded cotton scarves knotted around their necks. The paisley pattern had faded to a faint, solid color of grayish-blue. The old man wore new overalls with no shirt; the legs were rolled up to his bony knees. The old woman wore a homemade cotton floral print shift with the long sleeves pushed to her elbows. It was her underslip, usually worn under another cotton, winged loose dress and belted with a yarn or beaded leather belt. The old woman pointed to the bucket of diapers.

"Mee yahnish?" The Yakama word meant small child, or baby.

"Eeh." (Yes.)

I nodded my head up and down, pointing to our camp with my lower lip. She nodded her head, showing that she understood me. I was far from fluent in the Yakama Shahaptian language, but I understood a few basic words from hearing it spoken by Dad, relatives, and tribal members for most of my life on the Yakama Indian Reservation.

I also paid close attention when Mamma and my aunts spoke their Colville language because sometimes they talked about me! I was very surprised one day because suddenly I understood what they said. Aunt Susy told Mamma in Colville (Salish) it looked to her like I was really mad about something. Ever since I was a small child, both tribal languages sounded like music, beautiful and special; it was ours.

The old couple looked at each other and smiled whimsically, maybe remembering when they had their own babies and rinsed diapers in this same river. The old woman went to their pick-up and came back with an oblong, blue paper box of hard-tack crackers and a jar of homemade huckleberry jam, most likely her own. She put two heaping spoons of jam on one, spreading it around, and offered it to me. My mouth was already watering as I put out my hand for the snack. Grinning, the old man playfully reached in front of my hand for the cracker. The old woman slapped his hand away, making a noise and frowning while scolding him in their Yakama language.

"*Shu wowh, seeyewch!*" (Old fool, stop it!)

She gave me the hard tack, then we all broke out laughing heartily as I ate the offering. They gave me a cold bottle of Hires root beer from their old-fashioned metal ice chest, with a bottle cap opener welded to the side. The old man drank black coffee from a red metal thermos, sharing it with his wife.

The three of us sat quietly in the bright, warm sunlight on a blanket and looked out at the mirror-surfaced river. We watched a tugboat tow a large barge going west down the river. Small rippling waves billowed out behind the barge. We listened to the noisy seagulls as the waves started splashing gently on the sandy shore just below our feet. The smell of diesel smoke from the tugboat, wet driftwood, and dead, decaying salmon that had washed ashore on the waves was heavy in our nostrils. The old woman, her eyes closed, was softly chanting a song that I heard during Sunday services in the longhouse. The old man nodded his head as she sang. We were at peace with life and spiritually close to each other in those few moments. I still cherish the nearness I shared with those elders that day on the bank of the Columbia River.

Following the Colville custom, I shook their hands and pointed to the bucket then farther down the river, where I planned to rinse the diapers. They clasped both of their soft, wrinkled warm hands around mine, then stepped back, smiling, their brown arms around each other's waists, and watched me walk away. With his free hand, the old man held up the salmon with his fingers under the gills.

When I got back to camp; Dad was putting Joyce into her canvas car seat, the kind that hooked over the front seat, and reading a list from Mamma of what she wanted him to bring to the hospital. He took the rinsed diapers from my hand and put them into a plastic-lined wicker laundry basket in the trunk next to a large box of feathery soap flakes and bleach.

I sat next to the door in the front seat, which was a big honor for me. I kept my back ramrod stiff and looked straight ahead, moving a gigantic wad of bubble gum around in my mouth with my tongue. I didn't get to sit in the front very much. Joyce wiggled in her canvas chair between Dad and me, eating baby toast because she was teething. A couple of times I had to pull her back into her chair, because she was always trying to crawl out. On the way to the hospital I asked Dad when my baby brother could go swimming. I told him I already showed Joyce how to hum so she knew how to go underwater without getting water in her nose. He looked at me, shocked.

"Joyce can go underwater? Hey now, I don't want you drowning her, hear? You have to remember, Annie Lou, she's just a baby yet. Where is your mother when you have Joyce in the water?"

"Well, she's usually busy washing clothes and diapers or something, but she can do it, Dad. Joyce really likes the water."

As young as I was, somehow, I knew I had said too much.

"I'm going to have a talk with your mother about this, I just don't think babies should be in the river that soon, except to wash or to cool them off. Don't do that anymore, okay?"

"Uh huh."

I was playing peek-a-boo with Joyce when Dad said, "Well, here we are at the hospital. I'll take you and Joyce into the waiting room because kids aren't allowed to visit. Then I'll go upstairs and get Mamma and Earl Junior. Don't touch anything, or let Joyce scream around now."

I was pulling Joyce, whimpering, from under the glass coffee table by her tiny ankle when Dad came and told me to follow him, Mamma, and Earl Junior to the car. I hurried to get a look at the baby; Dad sat Joyce on his shoulders and a nurse pushed Mamma in the wheelchair. Looking tired but happy, Mamma lifted a corner of the little Pendleton woolen blanket from the cradleboard so I could see our new baby. He looked so small, and wrinkled like a brown prune. I had to ask Mamma about him.

"Was he already in water? When can I take him swimming? I can tell he'll really like the water, like Joyce. I just know it."

Oh-oh! I quickly skipped ahead to the car, ignoring

Dad's stern, warning look. I knew he was still mad about putting Joyce in the deep water with me. On top of everything, I had to ask if I could put the new baby in the river, right in front of Dad. *I'll never learn. I'll probably get a whipping or something worse later.* I could hardly wait to get back to Celilo, so I could go swimming with my friends for the rest of the day. It would probably be my last time.

4
Kuthla Smiled at Me

The Columbia River was a source of solace as well as the greatest joy for me. When I was scolded or spanked, I wouldn't cry until after I went swimming. I'd dive headlong into the water with my eyes open, making my eyes puffy and red to hide my tears. Any other time I swam just to feel happy, free, and carefree when I was in the river with my playmates.

"Hi, Kuthla,* hi."

The old lady above us was walking on the railroad tracks to her house. She wasn't my relative, but all the kids called her "Kuthla."

On this July day, the temperature was in the three digits and whole families were at the river, cooling off. Some were having picnics, washing clothes, and having swimming races or games. Even toddlers were in the water, splashing by their watchful parents. Mamma would probably be here later with my little sister and brother. Dad and my uncles, Joe and Jimmy, fished all day on their scaffolds at the falls. Sometimes they swam at night, after they got home, to relax and get clean. Dad told me once that the river was his private pool in those days.

*Kuthla, maternal grandmother in the Yakama language.

Kuthla hardly ever smiled at kids, even her relatives' kids. But that day she looked down at me in the water because I made such a racket and the tiniest hint of a smile lifted the corners of her lips. She didn't wave back, though. I felt good anyway because Kuthla actually, well sort of, smiled at me. I dove backwards into the river. Submerged in the water, I felt the thunderous rumbling vibrations the train made as it went by. I shot out of the water, wondering what it was that didn't seem right about that train . . . it didn't blow its whistle!

People started running to the very spot where I had just seen Kuthla when she stopped and looked down at me. A neighbor threw a blanket over something up there, I couldn't see what because it was out of my range of sight. The Yakama tribal police came with their sirens as did the county sheriff and an ambulance. I knew what happened to Kuthla! I couldn't move because my legs froze. I stood there in the river up to my chest in a kind of trance.

Everybody started getting out of the water. Families, people I knew gathered their blankets, towels and children together and left quickly, one by one. Still, I stood in the water, unable to move. The ambulance put the bloody blanket on a gurney and sped away. People were looking around where Kuthla was walking. I saw Wanda's mother, Nancy, pick up Kuthla's dusty beaded bag with a few cans, wilted celery and carrots sticking out of the top. Kuthla had been going home to make stew.

I don't remember when the last person left from up there on the tracks. I don't remember much of anything for hours. All of a sudden my head was shaking hard, I was shivering violently from being in the water for so long. I looked around, dazed, and realized it was dark, so I dipped my fevered face and head in the river and weakly made it to shore. I was so drained of strength; I couldn't even squeeze the snap on my jeans or pull up the zipper.

I staggered up the hill to our cabin carrying my clothes, and gobbled up the first thing I could find in the ice chest; a half pint of cottage cheese, and sliced baloney. It was late, and everybody was asleep or gone. Mamma and Dad were doing what they could to help Kuthla's family by going with them to the police station and then to the mortuary funeral home in The Dalles. I was forgotten in the chaos after what happened to Kuthla, they thought I was sent with the other kids to the neighbors. I drank a quart jar of water from the water can and finished the cottage cheese and baloney. I woke up late the next afternoon on Mamma's bed with the empty tub of cottage cheese and red, stringy baloney casings on my chest. Someone had covered me with a blanket, I started crying because I remembered the neighbor lady, Florence, putting a blanket over Kuthla. Mamma came to check on me.

"Oh, Annie Lou, you're awake. What's wrong, why are you crying, honey?"

"I'm (sob) feeling sad 'cause Kuthla smiled at me before she was run over, and that train didn't even blow its whistle, Mamma."

Mamma took me in her arms while I cried.

For a week I had bouts of crying and couldn't hold anything down, and my head felt hot all the time. I got delirious and weak and couldn't walk or stand up; I had to be carried to the outhouse. That's when my parents took me to the hospital in The Dalles, but the white doctors said there wasn't anything wrong with me. The nurses treated me for dehydration, putting me on IVs for a few hours then sent me home. When I still couldn't eat or stay awake, Dad took me back, but the white doctors said the same thing. At home in Celilo, I had crying bouts for hours and almost hiccupped to death one night. Finally, Mamma sent for her Uncle Johnny on the Colville Indian Reservation at Nespelem, Washington, over three hundred miles away north in Washington. Mamma's uncle was an Indian healer. He arrived at Celilo the next night. The first thing he did was put me on a reed pallet on the dirt floor and covered me with a soft buffalo robe, I was so cold, I couldn't stop shivering and crying.

For three days, Uncle Johnny or *Kowah*[*] woke me to drink sips of horsemint tea, and warm sarvice berry soup thickened with flour, I drifted in and out of sleep. He softly chanted songs that sounded to me like babbling creeks and the high-pitched voices of Eagle and Hawk all blending together.

He beat on a small drum that made me dream that my heart was pumping blood into the Columbia and back into my body. In that dream the Columbia River was red, and my own blood was clear green, like the river. In my state of delirium as I was seeking comfort, all I could think of was how I stood in the clear, green river when I grieved for Kuthla. The red blood was something out of my earliest memories from what my mother told me on the banks of the Columbia River when I was five years old as I watched the blood from the cut on my hand drip into the river.

I felt better by dawn on the third morning, I was weak but the dizziness was gone. I called for Mamma and she came, wearing her long-sleeved nightdress, carrying a tray. I looked at her and wanted her arms around me, I smiled, with tears flowing down my cheeks.

"Well, Annie Lou, how are you? You're smiling, so

---

[*]<u>Grandfather</u> in the Colville Indian language.

that's a good sign, eh *Kowah*?" She smiled at her Uncle Johnny, and he nodded his head slowly.

"*Key wah!*[*] It was a good healing spirit ceremony, it took a lot out of me, but we are all feeling happy now that Annie Lou is back with us. I thank the Creator."

Mamma nodded her head and started spoon feeding me more sarviceberry soup, but I sat up weakly and took the spoon and ate all the soup by myself. I didn't feel cold anymore and pushed the robe away. I stood up shakily and gave *Kowah* a hug, I cried into his shoulder, sobbing.

"Oh, *Kowah*, I wanted to get to know Kuthla better. I wanted to talk to her and sit by her feet to listen to her tell stories. I didn't want her to go up to the sky to the Creator yet. She smiled at me."

Kowah cradled me in his arms like an infant, making a clucking sound, consoling me.

"Grandchild, we can't choose who we want to travel home to the Creator or to stay here with us little longer. We don't have that right and never will. Only the Creator decides those things. We can only thank him for each day and live our lives the best way we can. You'll find answers during your lifetime, I have a few yet to find, and I'm old now. Get well for now, and help your mother with the little ones."

---

[*]Yes, in the Colville Indian language.

5
I Will Always Fear Rodents

I sat alone at the table, the last one, dawdling. I didn't want to eat my half-cup of peas, and waited for Aunt Susy's dog Ozzie to come by my feet so I could give him the disgusting green stuff. Dad said I wasn't to leave the table until I had eaten all my peas. I tried a spoonful, but spit them back out one at a time. Dad was reading the paper at the other end of the homemade table, waiting for me to finish. I looked sadly at Mom washing dishes; she purposely ignored me. I tried to pretend I was falling asleep so I would be sent to bed, but Dad rapped me painfully on the head with his finger.

"Now Annie Lou, that won't work, you're going to finish or else." He patted his belt buckle menacingly.

Ozzie entered the room, yawned and flopped down by the stove. Without moving my head, I looked to my right over the table at the dog, then left, sideways, at Dad. I patted my knee under the table, trying to get Ozzie's attention. He opened his eyes, jerked his head up and looked under the table at my legs. He made a little yip, making Dad look up from his paper at the dog then suspiciously at me. I grabbed the salt shaker and innocently seasoned my peas; I mashed about four or five with my fork and tried eating them that way . . . Ewwh! Yuck! I spit them back on the plate, scraping my tongue with my fingers, making me gag and cough.

Finally Ozzie got up and ambled under the table. I kept

an eye on Dad and dropped some of the peas off my fork to the dog. He sniffed at the nauseous green stuff and walked away. Darn traitor! Heck, I'd seen him eat rotten stuff, even poop for Pete's sake. I gave him an angry kick and he flopped down and started yelping like I had just stomped on his darn leg. Mom rushed over and lifted up the tablecloth to see what was wrong with that stupid dog, then Dad got up and went and stood beside her. Both bent over, looking under the table at poor Ozzie. He saw the forkful of peas on the floor and the five mashed ones still on my plate and then looked at me sternly. Mamma stood up and pursed her lips, putting both hands on her hips. I flinched as Dad rolled up his paper and swatted my arm and barked at me, "Oh for . . . just get your butt to bed!"

I bolted.

It was about nine o'clock at night that summer, and I sure didn't want to go back inside the lean-to kitchen to get my bright eel-fishing flashlight and have to look at Dad, so I made my way in the dark to the cabin and my mattress bed on the floor. In the dark I punched my pillow a few times to get it just right and bunched myself into the blankets. I was asleep before my parents came to bed with the babies.

"Ouch! Shit, that hurts!"

I turned my head and rubbed at the stinging, sharp pain on my left earlobe. In the dawn's dim light I saw a huge rat on my chest with small, eyes glittering like tiny flashlights! The rodent jumped off my chest, down to the floor and I heard it skitter along the wall and run out of sight. I pulled the quilt tightly over my head and curled into a fetal position in case there were any other rats. Then Dad jerked off my cover.

"What did you just say, young lady?" Grabbing my shoulder; his other hand was raised, ready to paddle me.

"Dad, a rat just bit me on my ear. Am I going to die from an infection?" I started crying, genuinely terrified.

"Omigod! Earl, what did she say?"

Mamma got up, pulled on her robe, and lit the kerosene lamp, bringing it over to Dad and me. I felt the sticky wetness on my cheek and neck, so I knew I was bleeding my life away. I begged Mamma for soap and water so I wouldn't die from the rat's infection that was speeding to my heart. Dad lifted me onto their bed and started getting dressed.

"We're taking her to the emergency room, NOW."

At The Dalles hospital the white doctors had the nurse clean the wound with a soft brush and antiseptic, then he gave me three stitches. For pain, I had some whiffs of awful-smelling ether, through a mask which terrified me, strapped over my face. I couldn't pull the mask off because they wrapped a sheet over my arms, holding them at my sides. I was crying real hard because I thought I was going to die for sure. I imagined a rat jumping out of a cupboard in the sterile white emergency room and biting me again while I was trussed up on that stretcher. After that experience, I couldn't stand the smell of hospitals for years. They kept me overnight to make sure I was out of danger. The doctor told Dad to bring me back if the bite wound got worse in any way.

Within two days my ear puffed up to twice its size, so I had to go back to the hospital and take a series of painful shots as a precaution against rabies. The tests they took were sent to a Portland medical lab and sent back ten days later. They showed I didn't have rabies.

The same summer, my friend, Beverly got bit on her upper lip by a rat and it puffed up too. But she never saw a doctor and was all right. I told her it puffed up because earlier, she laughed at my big ear.

Ever since then I have this phobia about any kind of rodents. Once, some one put a live ferret on my shoulder as a joke; my blood pressure shot up and I fainted. That one little vicious rodent at Celilo took something away from me. I used to empty dead mice from small traps and big rat traps all the time; I even wanted cute, little spotted gerbils from The Dalles Pet Shop the previous month. Before the rat incident, I felt I was more like a normal kid then, not deathly scared of rodents. Never again though.

6
Snake, Annie Lou!

During the night I put cedarwood kindling into the glowing fire under the fresh salmon hanging on poles suspended from ropes. I had watched Mamma and Aunt Susy every day this week, fillet and pierce the salmon with cedar sticks to hang for drying. We made a low, mostly smoky fire under the fish each night. I was told to watch the smoldering wood so that it wouldn't spark up any flames and scorch the salmon. During windy days all the hinged shutters were left open so that the breeze coming from the Columbia River could dry the fish just right. It was torture each night for my eyes because the smoke made them puffy and red. I sure could eat the fish though, when it was kippered just right and we brought it out in the winter to cut up and boil with flour dumplings. We also ate it right off the dried skin like fish jerky, as a salty snack, with crackers. Mamma used brand-new galvanized aluminum garbage cans with the lids secured down to store the fish for winter.

When we got to sleep; it was on army surplus bunk beds in the other half of the room, which was separated by a wood plank wall. The fish-drying half of the room had a dirt floor because we built the small fish-smoking fires in there.

Most dwellings at Celilo had the drying shed connected to the living quarters like that. I was playing with Joyce and Earl Jr. on the floor one morning while the women were cooking breakfast in the separate lean-to kitchen outside. The men had been fishing all night and were going to come back for breakfast and rest pretty soon.

All of a sudden I heard my aunt Margaret yell, "Snake! Annie Lou, snake! Get the kids up on the beds, hurry! There's a big snake crawling through the house."

Quickly, I put the toddlers on the bed but Earl Jr. scooted back to the floor to get his plastic cowboys. I jumped down, putting one foot on the floor to get him and then I saw it, the huge, shiny, black snake under the bed with its ugly head raised, staring at my little brother! I still had my left foot on the lower bunk. I moved real fast, grabbed my brother's right ankle and arm, and swung him up on the top bunk then jerked my right foot up. I heard his little curly head thump against something and knew he'd start wailing. The big snake slithered slowly over the plastic cowboys, under the other bunkbed and disappeared. Trembling, I scrambled up to my little brother and saw the red welt on his forehead, but he was all right.

I was shaking like a leaf inside and crying harder than Earl Jr. I hugged him to me to quiet his crying, and to calm myself down. I couldn't control my sobbing, which made him cry all the harder. I found Earl's bottle and gave it to him, he wouldn't let go of my tee shirt and fell asleep clutching my sleeve with sobbing hiccups. What a sight we made.

Shortly after that, Dad and my Uncles Joe and Jimmy came home with my older cousins, Richard and Marcus and they checked the floors for us so we could get down. They still had their fishing rain gear on, olive boots, wading pants with suspenders and plastic hats. When Dad checked the floor under the metal bunkbed I was on, he reached up and gently squeezed my arm and ruffled sleeping Earl Jr.'s head, waking him up. Poor Dad looked so tired from fishing all night, I gave him a tearful, shaky smile.

Then we all had a hearty breakfast of baked salmon, boiled potatoes, fried eggs and pancakes. Dad starting teasing Mamma, and my Aunts Susy and Margaret because they were jumping around on the long table when they walked in! He nudged Uncle Joe's arm.

"I thought for sure my little woman and her sisters were going to perform a genuine Indian can-can dance for us, right there on the eating table. Did you see how lively they were stepping, Joe?"

"Yeah, I saw that. My Susy used to cut the rug pretty good in our younger days, *enit* dear?" My cousins, Richard and Marcus, laughed when Aunt Susy gave Uncle Joe a mean "not now" scowl.

Mamma and my aunts blushed behind their hands modestly then they threw their aprons at Dad, telling him to button it up! I wanted to throw my fork at him too, because it wasn't a laughing matter, I was still feeling scared inside, remembering how close I was to that ugly snake. But at the same time, I felt so safe with Dad home to protect us from everything.

7

River Rock Wars at Celilo Falls

I was walking to the river for my daily swim, carrying a towel, water goggles and an empty bread sack of saltines. Then I heard them, the Shoban Reservation boys from Ft. Hall, Idaho calling on my older cousins Richard, Marcus, and James to a rock fight just because they were from the Yakama Indian Reservation. I thought it was silly of them to fight just because they were from another reservation, heck, I was friends with everybody who swam in the Columbia River below our place. But I also knew it was a territorial thing with boys. I was counting how many guys were on each side and whom I thought was tougher when my cousin Richard yelled at me to get back home before I got hurt. I turned around to tell him to shut up when a smooth, gray, river rock bounced off the top of my head, leaving a three-inch bleeding gash. My other cousin Marcus called the rock thrower a son-of-a-bitch for hitting a kid, and hurled a rock, hitting him in the shoulder blade with a sound like "whump!" The boy had tried to turn his body to dodge the stone. The war was on!

As I sat in the middle of the dirt road crying and bleeding, the boys threw rocks back and forth at each other. It was over quickly when the Idaho boys said they gave up. Two other Yakama boys, Leroy and Eli, came running to help, from across the railroad tracks, so Idaho was outnumbered.

My cousins packed me back to the house, and told Mamma I was throwing rocks at some other kids and got hurt! Their lie got me into trouble. I got a severe verbal lashing from Dad after I got back from the doctor's in The Dalles, to get stitches. When Dad got mad and yelled at me for nothing, it broke my heart. I vowed to get back at my cousins, and even the score.

Richard had a new girlfriend. When my friends and I were spending our nickels at Don's stand for candy bars I saw them laughing and drinking pop in the shade of Wanda's tourist stand. The girl with Richard was petite and pretty with curled blue-black hair. She was wearing rolled-up jeans and a man's baggy white shirt with penny loafers. When she laughed, it reminded me of those tinkling wind chimes on our porch at Wapato. They must have been serious about each other because I'd never seen Richard act so nervous with a girl. I walked up to him and asked for a quarter. He fished out some change from his pocket and handed it to me, just to get rid of me I think. I couldn't help noticing the fading purplish bruises on his thin arms from that rock fight a few days ago. I looked at the girl and knew who she was: Idell, the girl who babysat for my Aunt Marge's babies.

I wanted to stick around and make Richard more mad, but my friends insisted that we leave before the next barge went by. We liked to watch our sand houses flatten out and disappear like magic from the waves the boat made; it was the highlight of our day. I said 'bye to Richard ever so sweetly, but he just glared at me and I giggled.

"That was for lying and getting me in trouble," I muttered under my breath to him, lightly touching the bandage on my head.

When we got to our sand sculptures, there were some kids stomping all over them. They were from the Warm

Springs Reservation in Oregon. We all stood face to face, glaring at each other with hostile eyes. A dark girl my size, came up and lifted her chin at me. I quickly accepted the challenge; butting my shoulder into her chest, we crashed into the edge of the river! I was losing badly when my friend Wanda said, "All right, we'll settle this with a rock right, damn it!"

The dark girl let me up and I kicked at her as we rolled away from each other. Both sides ran for cover, grabbing up good smooth rocks for throwing as we ran. Another rock fight was in progress! It was over when both sides decided to call it even, nobody was hurt too bad, but my head was bleeding a little; the bandage came off when I was fighting that dark girl. It didn't hurt, though.

One of the Warm Springs girls came over and wanted to look at my wound, then another, and another. Afterwards we all sat in a circle on the sand, passing around Hershey's chocolate candy bars and bottles of 7-Up and root beer. We bragged about every scar we got from previous rock fights, then we built new sand pillars with our new friends. After that we all stood back and watched waves from the passing barge wash them away, along with our anger.

8
The Drowning

It was a typical July day at Celilo Falls . . . very hot, in the high nineties. The grasshoppers were unusually noisy today, clattering like a den of rattlers. I walked across the tracks to play with my friends. They weren't home, so I decided to go for an all-day swim, that's where everybody was anyway. Mamma had washed and pin-curled my short hair and combed it out this morning but it went limp from my sweating head. She had Aunt Marge trim my hair short after they shaved a section to stitch the cut I got from my older cousin's rock fight. Aunt Marge had curled Cousin Larry's hair too, it hung in black, shiny ringlets to his waist. I wondered why she didn't just braid it like she always did. But he was only three years old and didn't care what his mom did to his hair yet. Her two older boys, Melvin and Reggie, wanted their heads shaved or cut short because of the hot weather. She had only boys so far and liked to style hair, so she curled her youngest son's long hair, and kept the rest of the family's hair trimmed.

There were a lot of kids swimming that day. I swam with one group until they had to leave, and joined another group that had just arrived.

Daniel and I were the better swimmers and went out pretty far one day, when other kids from shore started yelling about something floating by us. I treaded water and looked around, trying to look into the water. The glinting sun made it difficult to see, but there was a dark, almost shadow-like lump partly submerged floating in the clear, greenish, water close to us. I couldn't figure out what that awful odor was coming from the lump. It smelled rotten, but unlike the decaying fish smell I was familiar with. There were always dead fish on the river banks. We both grabbed a hold of what felt like slippery, slimy skin and towed the lump to shore. When our feet touched the sandy bottom, we turned the lump over. It was a human in full fishing gear; his hands and face were drained of color, partially eaten away, and swollen beyond recognition. I gasped and put my hand over my mouth in shock. I got out of the water, gathered my shoes and clothes and told Daniel I was going home because I felt weird. I ran, stumbling over the hot sand and rocks, to the cabin and told my mom that we found a drowned fisherman. I said it was a white person. She drove off to let the police know. Later, I saw all the curious people and police cars with their flashing lights at the spot, but I couldn't bring myself to go back down to the river. It was over two weeks before I went swimming again, but I didn't go out as far as I usually did the rest of that summer. I became somewhat afraid of deep water, this fear started with the Columbia River at Celilo Falls, Oregon that summer.

The police came and talked to me at the cabin, but I didn't help them much, I mumbled barely audible answers to their questions. They gave Daniel a fifty-dollar reward. I refused to talk about what we found. Daniel talked freely about the body and was most helpful to the police, I guess it's because boys have more courage than girls do about those things. A few days later Daniel bought me a bottle of Hires root beer and a jawbreaker from the tourist stands with the money his mother gave him out of the reward.

After that day when we found that white man's body, I

would go and sit on the bank of the Columbia River and stare for hours out into the depths of the water looking for answers to questions I had about death. I loved feeling free and light when I swam and dove as deep as I could, but that was before I had any idea about what mammoth secrets were beneath or within the Columbia River. I was rudely awakened to the respect this wondrous river commanded just from my double experience with death at Celilo Falls. I became spiritually ill when Kuthla was run over by the train practically in front of my eyes, the river helped me with closure then. I developed a fear for the deep part of the water that I couldn't see into after Daniel and I pulled that drowning victim from the river.

Today, I would love to swim in the Columbia River every day of my life, eat fresh salmon with bitterroots, huckleberries, and drink spring water if I could. My life's trail will always lead me back to Celilo Falls.

9
Salmon Feast at Celilo Falls

It was early spring, time for the feast of the first foods: baked salmon, boiled bitter roots, and wild carrots, with frozen huckleberries and chokecherries thawed from last fall. The women elders gathered their digging irons, root bags made from corn husks wrapped around string, and woven tightly. Some of the older bags had elaborate geometric designs, made by dying the husks various colors of the earth; warm reds, browns, yellows, and blues. I always got a plain, colorless bag to tie around my waist, and I usually filled mine first, before the other girls. I thought that was unfair, but I was taught to keep quiet, not to ever talk back to any elders. I had been punished enough times to remember that! We all had to wear traditional cotton wing dresses and moccasins; the elders were strict about that.

The previous weekend before the Salmon and Root Feast, we went to the greening foothills on the Yakama Indian Reservations to look for roots. Before we started digging, the head woman sang the proper songs and rang a small hand bell rhythmically. The song carried over the ground, greeting and thanking the first roots for giving the real humans such a wonderful gift. After the ceremony, we smaller girls roamed all over the hills, digging and stopping to pick wild buttercups and bluebells to take back to our mothers. They usually got limp, but our mothers always gushed over them anyway to make us feel proud of ourselves.

After digging all morning and early afternoon, we went back to the Celilo Wyam longhouse. We were too small to help with the cooking, but we sat in a circle outside with the women and helped peel the huge mound of roots, then we washed all the reddish dirt off before they were simmered in huge cooking pots. The kitchen smelled so good. There was roasted venison, roots, berries, and fry bread. The cooking had been going on all morning, we could hardly wait to eat.

The boys served the venison and salmon, setting platters on the tables, then girls brought out the roots and berries, arranging them in the order that they came. The boys wore beribboned colorful shirts and moccasins; the girls wore wing dresses, moccasins, and braids if their hair was long enough. My hair was short, but Mamma put a small eagle fluff in my beaded barrette.

We finally got to sit down to eat, after all the prepared food had been set out on the tables and a prayer of thanks had been offered. When the leader told us to drink our water, we could eat. I had to sit in the kitchen with the other kids because there were a lot of people and visitors, all the tables were full. The tribal longhouse was big with many long tables, but it was still crowded. I dished out dumplings from the serving bowl of boiled salmon heads and put the fish cheek back into the bowl for somebody else. We were a noisy bunch and the elder whip man kept coming over to our table and shushing us, threatening to take us outside for a whipping. Each tribe has a whip man, to maintain discipline because parents can't watch their children all the time. The whip man has permission to keep all children in line. He would always tell you why you're being punished before the whipping. In earlier times parents would arrange for the whip man to come to their house to administer spankings, just to remind the children to behave themselves at all times. The whip man was given gifts and fed before he left for other houses.

Back to the salmon feast . . . as we were eating and trying to bridle excess energy I put a fish cheek on the plate of my friend next to me, he put it right back on my plate and dared me to eat the eyeball, a special delicacy for the elders. I shook my head no, but the whole table of kids joined in, egging me on. We quieted down only until the whip man walked away again. I took the eyeball out of the socket with a fork, put it into my mouth and swallowed it real fast because I couldn't bring myself to chew it. The cheers got boisterous and the whip man looked over at our table sternly. He strode over and stood directly behind me.

"What's going on here? If you're done eating, drink your water and start clearing this table, then go and start washing dishes."

I was so scared I had trouble breathing, making it hard to finish swallowing the fish eyeball. I felt it start to come back up, so I gulped down my water. The eyeball popped out anyway and sailed across the table, hitting my friend Gladys on the cheek. She screamed and jumped up, rubbing her face hard with the back of her hand. I started laughing and gagging which made the other kids laugh all the more heartily, even though the whip man was standing right there!

The whip man put both hands on my shoulders and yanked me to my feet.

"Since you're always in the middle of everything, Annie Lou, I'll start with you. I want you all (pointing his bony finger at each one) to march outside and line up, *tuk tu* (hurry)!"

He gave each one of us a stern lecture before he used the willow switch on our mischievous backsides that day.

The people sitting at the tables, wondering what all the commotion was about coming from the kitchen, marched outside and watched. The crazy thing was this: even though we knew we would be in even bigger trouble with whip man, but whenever we looked at each other we couldn't help breaking into peals of insane giggles and laughter! My stomach hurt worse than my bottom when I got home and I got another paddling from Dad for being bad at the feast.

As I remember those days at Celilo Falls, I can actually see myself in my children and now my grandchildren as they grow. I will always be there.

10
Swimming in the Rain

I woke up and as usual, the first thing I did was look out the window to see what the weather was like. At ten o'clock in the morning it was overcast and partly cloudy, with patches of blue sky, so that meant it wouldn't rain until later in the afternoon. I could get in a morning swim easy. I knew Mamma had a salmon waiting for me to clean for the evening meal. I went down to the lean-to kitchen and looked in the stove warmer for something to eat, splashed water on my face, ate a pancake-and-bacon sandwich, then brushed my teeth.

I looked in the wooden fish box, hooked my finger under the ice-packed salmon and headed for the river, with my fish-cutting knife and spoon. *I'll bring the salmon back before I swim, that way I won't have to deal with the seagulls and dogs bothering the fish and eggs while I swam.* Aunt Marge was there at the river that morning, washing diapers, her newborn was in a baby sling on her back. The new baby was a beautiful, black-haired little girl named Janice, her first daughter. I didn't even know she was going to have this baby.

I cleaned the fish and took it back to the cabin. After I iced down the fish again, my cousin Melvin came out of the house and said he'd go swimming with me. He didn't swim as much as I did, and he liked to swim when there weren't so many people around. We were opposites, I liked to be around lots of friends; he liked to be with very few people at any time. He told me he was going to swim alone today, but he knew I would swim come rain or shine, so he decided to join me. When we got to the swimming spot, a warm wind started up and the skies darkened. I dove in and splashed around for almost a half-hour before Melvin dove in with his blue jeans on. I thought to tell him that blue jeans took on about five to six pounds of water weight when soaking wet, but I figured he knew that and wouldn't swim out too far. Being himself, Melvin wouldn't listen anyway, he'd just do the opposite to prove me wrong on anything. Boys!

I was doing backstrokes, back flips, and just horsing around in the water when I heard a sound like a loud gargle. I looked for Melvin and saw him way out. Swirling water was coming from beneath the surface and I knew right away that he was caught by a strong undertow. I yelled at him to swim hard toward the shore and to me but he panicked, too terrified to understand me.

"Help me, Annie Lou, help me!"

When I saw his terrified, bloodshot eyes I knew he was in trouble. Without thinking, I swam out to him. When I got to him I grabbed both sides of his face and tried to calm him down.

"Get on your back, just float on your back to save strength, I'll pull you."

Between gulps of air, I tried my hardest to get those words out, but he misunderstood me and tried to *crawl on my back,* pushing my head underwater! Then I got scared that he'd drown both of us and I swallowed a lot of water trying to tell him to get on his back and stay afloat myself at the same time.

When I knew Melvin wasn't hearing a word I was trying to say I decided to do something he wouldn't suspect. I brought my right arm back and punched him in the face as hard as I could against the splashing water. He gasped and froze in shock, when I felt him go limp, I grabbed his hair and started kicking backward to the shore. When I felt sand under my feet, I put my arm under Melvin's and let go of his hair. I gave a cry of relief and the tears flowed freely from my eyes, like the steady pouring summer rain. I pulled him onto the sand and rolled him from side to side until he coughed up and vomited most of the water he swallowed. He lay face down with forehead on his arms for awhile, then I helped him sit up and wrapped him in his tee shirt and my sweatshirt because he was shivering and his teeth chattered with a chill. I wrapped our towels around him too, and helped him walk back up to the house for hot chocolate and graham crackers.

    We sat across from each other at the table and drank several cups of the sweet hot liquid, not saying a word, just smiling weakly at each other. We never told our folks what happened, because I didn't want to jeopardize my daily swim, and Melvin didn't want to be reminded of how dumb he was to swim in his blue jeans. I was the only one to ever tease him about it, but after that, he never got too mad at me about anything again.

11
They Took Our Thunder

It was March, 1957, the Columbia River began to cover the ancient fishing site at Celilo Falls when gigantic floodgates closed at the newly built Dalles Dam, eighteen miles to the west, downriver. I was there with my family above Wishram, Washington, across from Celilo Falls—we watched the water rise until the falls was completely immersed and there were only swirling dimples in the water where Celilo Falls had been and our house had stood. The river then smoothed out, continuing on its path west, to the Pacific Ocean as it had done for hundreds of years.

Tribal members watched from Washington and Oregon shores as the river rose slowly over the historic landmark, immersing it forever.

After Celilo Falls was completely covered by the Columbia River, we were all quiet for a few minutes, each one of us in deep thought. I looked up to watch an eagle fly overhead in a circle, higher and higher into a brilliantly blue, cloudless sky. Then one of the elders in front of us rose from his Pendleton-blanket-covered chair. Using his cane to turn around and face the people, he spoke in the Shahaptian Yakama language in a quavering voice.

"Remember this day, all of you young ones here, when they took away our Celilo Falls . . . just like you would say, they took our thunder. Aih-h-h." He raised his right hand and turned to the left in a complete circle.

With head bowed, the elder's thin shoulders shook, his tears flowed like the Columbia. He was overcome with his sorrow, our sorrow. Looking around, I witnessed salmon fishing tribes: the Yakama, the Umatilla, the Nez Perce, and the Warm Springs men and women as they wept openly, which in turn, made me cry. I was too young to understand that the strange, aching heaviness in my chest was a breaking heart. I remember crossing and holding my arms tightly, trying to understand and soothe the grievous, crushing pain. It felt like I had broken ribs, but more painful.

Many months before, the Yakama tribe's enrolled elders and descendants who were twenty-one years old, voted and agreed to allow the dam to be built by the government, knowing it would end salmon fishing at Celilo Falls for eternity.

I had so many fond memories of my childhood summers from the late 1940s to the mid 1950s spent in the fishing village known as Celilo Falls; recollections meant to be shared with my future children and grandchildren.

By treaty rights the Yakamas and their enrolled descendants from the Umatilla, the Nez Perce, and the Warm Springs tribes could still fish below and above The Dalles and Bonneville Dams during set seasons. Each Yakama tribal member was awarded three thousand dollars, because they had been fishing at the site the longest, for hundreds of years. It took our family fishing for months to make that much money. We generally received a few hundred dollars from the sale of one pick-up load of salmon on a good day. Three thousand dollars was a lot of money to have all at once, and the younger adult tribal members didn't hesitate to sign I heard the elders say. Most Native Americans I knew had families with four or more children and bills at the age of twenty-one so the money didn't go very far.

My mother was a full-blood, Colville Indian, and my biological father was a full-blood, Spokane Indian. My grandparents and ancestors were from these Salish-speaking plateau tribes and Indian reserves in British Columbia, Canada. Knowledge of our heritage was one of the traditional teachings and important for Indian children to know, because then they always knew who they truly were. It has always been our way of life as far as I understood.

My stepfather, Earl Wahpat Sr. (Dad) and my little half-sister Joyce, and brother Earl Jr., were enrolled Yakamas. My mother married Earl when I was almost two years old. Joyce and Earl Jr. were too young to remember much of Celilo. I was the one who taught them to tread water by dog paddling, and to hold their breath underwater by humming (Earl Jr. preferred to blow bubbles) while they were still in cloth diapers. Because of that early connection with the Columbia River they were never afraid of water and knew how to swim at an early age. Today they look at our old snapshots of Celilo with a look of wonder and smile. I look at the same pictures with acute sadness followed by tears, because I can remember who took most of those snapshots with our old box camera. Our parents and older relatives are gone now, those snapshots and my memories are all we have left.

I will always think of Celilo Falls, Oregon when I see white people in belted, Madras plaid Bermuda shorts. They wore the current style of printed or solid, cotton short-sleeved shirts with white tee shirts underneath. The women wore jeans and shorts with buttons and zippers on the left side. Today's style is tank tops and tee shirts in every color imaginable and ragged cut-off denims with everything.

When I was a child at Celilo Falls, we lived southeast, just above Celilo Falls in a cluster of temporary Indian homes built to live in only during the late spring and summer fishing seasons.

One year our camp was flooded when I was five, so that summer my room was the bed of our half-ton Ford truck with a huge brown, oily tarp tied down over the wooden side racks. It was the best room I ever had. At night the stars winked at me from between the racks and sometimes soft summer rain pelted the tarp in a musical, lulling rhythm before I feel asleep. Sometimes, during the night I'd wake up and watch the neighbors, who were illuminated by kerosene lamps and outdoor fires as they sat on their summer furniture of wooden boxes or canvas-covered folding chairs. They would be drinking beer, cussing at the barking dogs, cooking, talking and laughing amongst themselves. They talked and joked with the other neighbors in the dark night. They couldn't actually see each other in the dark, but they knew everybody by their voices. I learned from listening to their conversations about my friends' parents who had "torn the blanket," meaning they broke up or separated over the weekend. I also knew those parents always got back together by the middle of next week because they had a lot of kids to take care of. I heard that two women we knew, who lived across the tracks, were expecting babies again (they had the biggest families, ten and twelve children respectively). A celebration was coming up on the Warm Springs Indian Reservation in Oregon. There was going to be a big give-away and name-giving ceremonies after a wedding at Klickitat, Washington at the Spino's home. I knew who caught the most salmon and how many pounds they got on an island of rock called Chief Island, where my stepfather had his fishing scaffold. Mamma always wondered where I heard the gossip before she and her sister, my Aunt Susy Joe did!

All of our houses sat side-by-side in a crooked line going up a low hill. The road was a well-traveled dusty dirt lane with short driveways in front of each residence. The houses were built to live in temporarily during the summer. Most places, like our first house, had wooden floors with three to four feet-high walls and a hinged door. On top of this structure, a white or olive army canvas tent was securely attached. A large lean-to was added with a huge, wood-burning stove for cooking. The lean-to was the "kitchen" where we kept an ice-filled small fridge (a block of ice kept in the top compartment) for our perishable food, and huge wooden lockers for dishes, canned goods and staples. We sat and ate on homemade tables and benches. There was always a big gray, speckled metal pot of strong coffee sitting on the back of the stove. For light we used kerosene lamps. A few years later Dad put in electricity wires for electrical outlets and lightbulbs. Some families built sturdy regular wooden houses on higher ground, if they lived at Celilo Falls the year round. The Bureau of Indian Affairs built long concrete buildings with separate family housing units next to the rocky hill across the highway, but you had to sign up early to get one of those.

Dad was a combination fisherman, hunter, self-taught mechanic, electrician, and carpenter so he built our cabins himself. He also built our two-story house where we lived and went to school on the Yakama Indian Reservation at Wapato, Washington. When we weren't fishing, whole families did seasonal labor in and around the agricultural Yakima Valley in Washington and Oregon. After school it was my job, because I was the oldest girl, to watch over the smaller children and start dinner for our working parents. All I could do until I learned to cook was peel potatoes and make a small fire in our kitchen wood stove to start water boiling in the coffee pot. As I got older, I had more responsibilities. Mamma said it was important for us girls to know how to take care of a house and kids when we grew up.

When we traveled to work we would set up camp to cook our stews and fry bread wherever the work was and I helped our parents in the hop and vegetable fields and fruit orchards. It was nomadic, and it was our way of life.

I met and made many lifelong friendships from other tribes and white kids from other parts of the United States whose families followed the crops and worked the year around to survive. These kids had traveled all over America and attended schools in just about every state. Later in the 1960s they were called gypsies and hippies, but I called them our friends.

When Dad built our cabins at Celilo, he bought what he needed from The Lumber & Building Supplies Store in The Dalles. That store had a large sign that said, FREE PUPPIES IN REAR. That meant we usually got a puppy whenever we went into The Dalles, west on Highway 84. I remember it was a two-lane highway, now it's a freeway with four lanes. A couple of my favorite dogs came from that lumber store. The first one I can remember is Spuddy, a small black-and-white rat terrier mixed with dachshund, I think. The other was a blond, peanut-butter-colored sheep dog we named Skippy (for the peanut butter). My little brother Earl and Cousin Reggie stubbornly called him Jiffy (for the other peanut butter), so that crazy dog answered to both names! One other dog I can remember was a large, playful reddish-brown boxer we named Butch. He got rabies and it broke my heart when he had to be put away. I can still see his sad, wet eyes looking at me when we drove away from home so I couldn't see my uncle loading his gun and when he buried Butch for us. Butch helped me learn to swim by letting me hold on to him in the deepest part of the water when we splashed around happily in the Columbia River.

The Northwest Union Railroad and Highway 84 went straight through the middle and upper south part of the Celilo Falls fishing village. There was another railroad below, closer to the river that went by just thirty yards from our cabin. There was a combination service station/restaurant/gift shop with a post office on the north side of the highway. Celilo Falls, in all its splendor, surged below the restaurant's picture window and gave travelers and tourists an impressive scenic view while they dined on twenty-five-cent hamburgers and two-dollar meatloaf and chicken dinners. I saw a number of photographers with sophisticated camera equipment take pictures of Celilo Falls for postcards, magazines and literary journals from that huge window. Celilo Falls was a gift from the Creator, a beautiful masterpiece of nature's wonder.

One summer my playmate, eight-year-old Daniel, fell into the falls from his father Don's scaffold. He was rescued from the swirling waters when he was caught in a steel-rimmed net by one of the Indian fishermen, Mr. Bushman. I saw that story with pictures of Daniel clinging to the net for dear life later that year in *LOOK* magazine. Daniel's near-drowning didn't scare me enough to stop my playing in the smooth, swift-running water just below the falls, where we caught eels after dark with strong flashlights. We used three-pronged hooks on eight-to-ten-foot poles tied on firmly with heavy-duty twine we used to weave fishing nets with. It was difficult to see the eels in the water during the day, so we usually caught them at night. The eel season ran in late spring and mid summer for a few days during both times. We hooked and pulled eels off the rock they clung to under the water with their mouth's strong suction and circular row of teeth in the swift flowing water. Some of the older kids used long wooden poles attached to small steel hoops with fine nets to go over the eel and under its head so they could be pulled off the rocks. It took strong arm and shoulder muscles to hold the long pole against the powerful, cascading water and then to work it over the eels and under their heads. That's why I preferred the three-pronged hook method. After catching one, we put the squirming eel in a gunnysack, but old pillowcases worked, then tied it shut because they wiggled and wrapped around your arm like thick, black snakes! They stopped moving around when they were out of the water awhile. The first time I was hooking eels and didn't know any different, my cousin, James Hunt Jr. told me to bite down on the white spot on the back of the head to kill them, he said it was the only way. I had to very carefully work that eel off my bleeding tongue before I could give chase and try to punch his face for that!

We eat eels in pretty much the same way as the Indians have for decades; roasted over open fires on split cedar sticks, which is my favorite. They're very oily, but the meat is very tasty. Some people I know don't like eels, it's an acquired taste I guess. We also broil them in the oven and dry or kipper the eels like salmon, over a low, flameless, smoky fire, to be eaten in the winter. They can also be cleaned, frozen fresh, thawed and broiled for feasts later. They always taste so good to me. Of course we have to have starchy dishes like potatoes, rice, and fresh fry bread or any kind of bread because of the rich oil. Dried salmon and eels are always a delicious snack with saltine crackers and a tall beverage. I know a few Indians who still remember those fresh eels from Celilo and lick their lips. Their mouths must be salivating like mine.

Celilo Falls was on the south side of the Columbia River directly across from the little town of Wishram, Washington. The river's northern border was smooth and swift with strong undercurrents. Looking above Wishram, is the highway with rolling, velvet-looking, pale golden hills. Railroad tracks went along the Columbia River on both shores, through Celilo Falls and Wishram. There was a railroad bridge that crossed the Columbia River a half mile west of Wishram and Celilo.

Sometimes, Dad or a group of dads would get "lost" and go drinking at the lone tavern in Wishram. They got over there by walking across that railroad bridge. Mamma and our aunts had to drive east to cross on the ferry boats at Biggs, Oregon or west at The Dalles to go after them! I remember watching Mamma and the other angry Indian women dragging their husbands out to the cars and trucks by their sweatshirt collar or braids!

I swam every day, even when it rained. I became part of the Columbia River from all that swimming and playing daily on its shores. It was my chore, as the oldest child of the family to clean a fresh salmon for our main meal every day. I took the salmon to the riverbank behind our house. After cutting off the head and slitting the salmon open, I removed the innards and scraped out the dark brown spine with a grapefruit spoon. I fed the guts to the numerous hovering seagulls. Those gluttonous birds would catch pieces in the air, or dive right into the river for them! Nothing was wasted and the gulls helped keep the river clean this way. Whoever was preparing the salmon saved the head for last to boil it like the salmon eggs. We always made these nutritious delicacies in thickened dumpling soups for the elders. I always jumped in the water for a short, cooling swim before taking the salmon back to Mamma to bake or she might fillet it for roasting over an open fire on sticks outside by the house. I couldn't swim very long because I had to keep chasing away pesky seagulls and hungry dogs from the salmon, head, and eggs.

To this day I still respect and take care of the Columbia River and never throw empty bottles, cans, wrappers, or cartons into the river or into any other body of water. I was taught that the Creator, water, and nature deserve the highest regard from us. The Columbia River helped me to see why; it's because they take care of us in turn.

I remember the spring when I was five and we moved earlier than usual to Celilo. I woke up one morning and everybody was excitedly bustling around fast and shouting in our tent. I sat up on the army cot I was sleeping on and saw muddy water, ankle deep and rising, on the floor! The murky water had debris, parts of trees and vegetation. It was early spring and the river was still getting the thaw from the mountains. This year we had set up our camp at another place downriver, below the railroad bridge, too close to the river for this time of year. I looked for my brown sandals and saw them floating near the tent door. Mamma shouted at us to hurry and pack whatever we could and get to higher ground. I heard other Indians from outside asking if everybody inside was okay. We carried what we could, climbed into the big Ford truck and Dad drove up to the highway. A few hours later the river crested and that's when I saw my big cloth doll, Sleepyhead, floating and bobbing away in the swollen river. Brokenhearted, I cried for my favorite doll and Mamma promised to buy me another one just like her. Now, I knew why I had dreamt of standing close to, almost <u>under</u> the Celilo Falls; it was the sound of the rushing flood waters creeping slowly up around us while we slept.

Before the tourists or anybody could go below the highway to park and watch the Indian fishermen at Celilo Falls, they had to drive or walk over a small wooden one-way bridge across a concrete canal used for small boats and barges to bypass the swift falls. Before going over the bridge, people stopped at one of the two small wooden buildings, with plastic-covered checkered counters, much like stands selling fireworks today on Indian reservations around the Fourth of July. White people owned these stands, selling cold drinks, grilled hot dogs, burgers, snacks, postcards, and beadwork made by local Indian women.

The two owners, a lady with dyed black hair named Wanda and a blond-headed man with black-rimmed glasses named Don, bought our beadwork to sell to tourists, with their other merchandise. Whenever they sold sunglasses or cold sodas they also sold a beaded item or two. My mother's little beaded Mickey Mouse and Donald Duck coin purses were in Don's stand; the first beadworked Disney characters I remember seeing. I still have one of Mom's little colorful Mickey Mouse purses; he looked like his Steamboat Willy character with stick arms and legs!

My favorite treat from Wanda's stand was one-cent white wax bottles filled with cherry syrup and a ten-cent cold bottle of Coke or Seven-Up. For five more cents, I bought Hershey's chocolate bars from Don's because he kept them chilled on a big block of ice. When I earned a quarter folding laundry or ironing wing dresses for my Aunt Susy Joe or two dollars hanging sixty-foot fishing nets on long raised, horizontal poles for Dad, that money went a long way! I always tried to put away a few silver coins though. The larger nets were used for fishing from small motorboats in smoother waters downstream (westward) toward The Dalles and Cascade Locks, near Bonneville Dam.

I know what other Indians are talking about when they talk about the tourists at Celilo Falls with their plaid Bermuda shorts and carrying box cameras hanging around their necks. I saw them too. They always went down as close as possible to the raging water to take pictures of Indians fishing at the falls as they netted salmon from wooden scaffolds with long wooden poles of pine or cedar, attached to eight- or ten-foot diameter steel-rimmed dip nets. The tourists always bought a fresh salmon that came straight from the river to take home packed in regular or dry ice. I'll never forget seeing how dry ice emits a weird, acrid-smelling white vapor. The smell gave me bad memories like the ether masks the Kushman hospital nurses strapped over my face when I had my tonsils removed at a Tacoma Indian hospital. I remember when I panicked and started kicking and thrashing frantically, trying to get away. The nurses roughly strapped down my arms with wide strips of cloth, instructing me to start counting from ten, but I screamed and struggled until I was unconscious from the ether.

The fishermen wore full rain gear and wading boots if they built scaffolds sites below the crashing falls because of the heavy mist the falls created, it was like a heavy tropical rainstorm. The ones who fished on their sites above the falls and out on the islands of rock wore regular clothes, hooded jackets with rain boots, because the mist was not so heavy, it was more like the fine spray I clearly remembered.

That cool mist was wonderfully uplifting and refreshing on my face in the three-digit summer heat. I recall watching a pretty, red-haired white woman using her husband's handkerchief to wipe off all her powder, rouge, and bright red lipstick after her face got wet from the mist. She held up her chin, facing the falls with her eyes closed, as if she were praying while the water powerfully rumbled in our ears. In that moment I understood one-on-one what she was feeling because I felt the same thing every day. I heard the power and felt the spirit of Celilo Falls talking to me, even in my sleep at night.

One day I was hurrying home from Dad's scaffold to

clean a sixty-pound salmon in a wet burlap sack for a birthday dinner when I overheard a pretty little blonde girl begging her dad (who was wearing Bermuda shorts) to take a picture of her and "that Indian girl with a big fishie in her sack" before they went home. I courteously stopped and stood waiting for him to snap a picture. I looked at the little girl; her skin was so white and pearly, just like the salmon's belly. She had on a pink ruffled gingham sleeveless blouse and shorts, with real nice white leather sandals. I was saving change whenever I could to buy a pair of canvas sandals like hers at the five and dime department store in The Dalles. Real leather, *sheesh*! I, on the other hand, wore a faded sundress, under a second or third generation hand-me-down flannel shirt with well-worn half melted plastic flip flops. Can you imagine how shoddy I felt at that moment?

I took the fish out of the gunnysack for the picture and when I held it up with three fingers, an idea popped into my head. I "accidentally" touched the little girl's thin, bare arm with the fresh, slimy salmon. She shuddered, then screamed, ruining the picture. I didn't understand why she was so scared, heck, the fish was flat-out dead! I did this "accidentally" a few more times to have some fun before her daddy finally took a good picture. Well, we saw that picture a year later as a four-cent postcard in the corner drugstore in The Dalles. I remember (with pride now) that I looked so solemn, dark, and wild next to that pretty, neat little blonde girl with her fish-belly white skin. That salmon didn't look too shabby either, I might add. Looking at that postcard, I remembered her father smothering a grin whenever his daughter screamed because he knew exactly what I was doing. I couldn't even force myself to smile for the camera and I didn't know why but today I understand. I remember thinking to myself, as I stood there holding up that heavy salmon measuring almost as tall as me, *I wish they'd hurry and take their pictures, because I should have cleaned this fish a long time ago, before the tongue turned that shade of pink. Mom's going to whip me, and then Dad will whip me because I fooled around too long.* That thought plainly shows in my poker straight face staring out from that postcard.

I have no idea where that postcard is today.

Those of us who had the job of cleaning a fish before meals, the eldest child, will readily understand that solemn look on my face in that postcard. How? Well, because we were all there, at Celilo, before the waters behind The Dalles Dam backed up and buried our thunder forever, like a gigantic beaver dam.